HOUSE OF ABUNDANCE PUBLICATIONS

Sailing Beyond the Horizon

Captivating Facts About Cruise Ships – A Deep Dive into the World of Maritime Leisure

Copyright © 2023 by House of Abundance Publications

All rights reserved. No part of this publication may be reproduced, stored or transmitted in any form or by any means, electronic, mechanical, photocopying, recording, scanning, or otherwise without written permission from the publisher. It is illegal to copy this book, post it to a website, or distribute it by any other means without permission.

House of Abundance Publications asserts the moral right to be identified as the author of this work.

House of Abundance Publications has no responsibility for the persistence or accuracy of URLs for external or third-party Internet Websites referred to in this publication and does not guarantee that any content on such Websites is, or will remain, accurate or appropriate.

Designations used by companies to distinguish their products are often claimed as trademarks. All brand names and product names used in this book and on its cover are trade names, service marks, trademarks and registered trademarks of their respective owners. The publishers and the book are not associated with any product or vendor mentioned in this book. None of the companies referenced within the book have endorsed the book.

First edition

This book was professionally typeset on Reedsy.
Find out more at reedsy.com

"A journey by sea is an adventure that awakens the soul and fills it with wanderlust."

- Unknown

Contents

1. Introduction — 1
2. Exploring the Foundations of Cruise Ship Engineering — 5
3. The Economic Impact of Cruise Ships — 16
4. The Environmental Impact of Cruise Ships — 22
5. Cruise Ships and Overtourism — 32
6. Maritime Safety and Cruise Ships — 40
7. Sunken Vessels: A Historical Perspective — 47
8. The Future of Cruise Ships — 54
9. Conclusion — 62

Call to Action — 64
Glossary of Nautical Terms — 66
Additional Resources for Further Reading — 67
Resources — 69

1

Introduction

Welcome aboard, adventurous readers, to a captivating voyage through the vast oceanic realm of maritime leisure. In this book, "Sailing Beyond the Horizon: Captivating Facts About Cruise Ships," we embark on a thrilling deep dive into the extraordinary world of cruise ships, where boundless horizons and unforgettable experiences await.

The allure of cruise ships has captured the imagination of humanity for centuries. From the early seafaring vessels of antiquity to the modern behemoths that traverse the seas today, these floating marvels have carried explorers, traders, and pleasure seekers to distant lands and beyond the horizon. With each passing year, cruise ships evolve, becoming increasingly sophisticated and luxurious, offering a compelling escape into a realm of boundless possibilities.

Our journey through these maritime wonders will take us on an enchanting exploration of the history, technology, and sheer grandeur that define these floating cities. From the momentous beginnings of cruise travel to the impressive engineering feats that underpin modern maritime giants, we will uncover the secrets of these oceanic behemoths and the intricate ballet of logistics that ensures smooth sailing.

Yet, this book is not just a technical guide or a dry compendium of facts; it is a celebration of the allure of cruise travel and its unparalleled experiences. We will delve into the enchanting world of onboard entertainment, gourmet dining, and leisure activities that transform each voyage into a floating utopia. As we navigate through the vibrant tapestry of onboard life, we'll uncover the magic that transforms these vessels into veritable floating cities, bringing together people from diverse backgrounds to share in the joy of discovery.

However, our exploration continues. Beyond the glitz and glamour, we will venture into the environmental impacts of cruise ships and the industry's relentless pursuit of sustainable practices. We'll examine how innovation and responsibility converge to ensure these magnificent vessels coexist harmoniously with the fragile ecosystems they traverse.

"Sailing Beyond the Horizon" is a tribute to the sense of wonder accompanying every journey in these oceanic palaces. Whether you are an experienced cruiser or a curious landlubber seeking to dip your toes into the vastness of maritime leisure, this book promises to enthrall and educate, offering a rich tapestry of tales and knowledge.

So prepare to cast off the shackles of the mundane and embark on a virtual adventure that will whisk you away to distant shores,

INTRODUCTION

where the sun-kissed waves beckon and the sea's mysteries unfold before your eyes. Welcome aboard as we set sail beyond the horizon, eager to uncover the fascinating world of cruise ships and the wondrous maritime escapades that await!

Brief History of Cruise Ships

Cruise ships have a long and storied history dating back to the mid-19th century. The concept of a cruise for pleasure was first introduced by Arthur Anderson and Brodie McGhie Wilcox, the founders of the Peninsular & Oriental Steam Navigation Company. However, it was the Pacific Mail Steamship Company, in 1840, that first advertised leisure voyages to the burgeoning middle class. Initially, these journeys were offered to transport mail and passengers. Still, they quickly grew in popularity as a novel form of recreation.

This chapter discusses the development of cruising from these humble beginnings, through the era of immigration voyages in the late 19th and early 20th centuries, to the birth of the modern cruise industry in the mid-20th century. It explores how technological advances, shifts in societal norms, and evolving travel trends have influenced the shape and scope of cruise ships and their experiences. It also presents a panorama of the transformative moments and key figures that have helped chart this industry's course.

Importance and Growth of the Cruise Ship Industry

From its early inception, the cruise ship industry has emerged as a significant player in the global tourism sector. As an intersection of transportation, accommodation, and entertainment, cruise ships offer a unique, all-inclusive travel experience attracting millions of vacationers annually. Over the decades, the industry has experienced robust growth fueled by various factors, including increased disposable income, changing demographic patterns, technological innovations, and tourism globalization.

This section discusses the importance of the cruise ship industry in the global economy, considering its direct and indirect impacts on job creation, revenue generation, and infrastructural development. It also examines the growth patterns in this sector, highlighting key statistics and trends from various regions around the world. Furthermore, it illuminates the industry's resilience in the face of challenges, discussing how it has weathered economic downturns, navigated changes in travel norms, and responded to crises.

2

Exploring the Foundations of Cruise Ship Engineering

Cruise ships, grand vessels that gracefully sail the vast oceans, are more than just opulent floating hotels. They are the extraordinary culmination of engineering marvels, applying intricate principles of shipbuilding to ensure safety, efficiency, and the seamless provision of services to thousands of passengers. In this section, we embark on a captivating journey into the fundamental principles that underpin the creation of these magnificent floating cities.

Buoyancy: Sailing on the Sea of Physics

At the heart of every ship's design lies the principle of buoyancy—an elemental force rooted in Archimedes' timeless discovery. The concept of buoyancy dictates that an object immersed in a fluid experiences an upward pressure equal to the weight of the fluid displaced by the object. Shipbuilders harness this fundamental law of physics to ensure that cruise ships float majestically atop the water's surface, defying gravity with an elegant equilibrium.

Intricately balancing the vessel's weight, shape, and structure, naval architects craft the hull to displace just enough water to maintain buoyancy. It is a meticulous dance of science and art, where the ship's draft—the vertical distance between the waterline and the keel—dictates the precise equilibrium needed for stable sailing. Thus, a well-designed hull efficiently glides through the ocean, cutting through waves with poise and providing passengers with a smooth and comfortable journey.

Displacement: Shaping Stability and Maneuverability

Cruise ships, with their imposing size and capacity, must grapple with the principle of displacement. This principle refers to the volume of water a ship's hull displaces when it floats. The shape and size of the hull significantly impact both stability and maneuverability, two vital aspects of the ship's performance.

Designers adopt various hull forms tailored to the ship's specific purpose and operating conditions. A bulbous bow, for instance, enhances hydrodynamic efficiency, reducing drag and improving fuel efficiency. Additionally, modern cruise ships may feature stabilizers and retractable fins beneath the hull that reduce rolling and improve passenger comfort during inclement weather.

By artfully manipulating displacement through ingenious hull designs, engineers optimize the ship's performance for safe and agile navigation, seamlessly navigating the most challenging waters with finesse.

Materials Science: A Symphony of Strength and Efficiency

Underneath the surface, the selection of materials plays a pivotal role in cruise ship construction. The hull, the ship's protective armor against the elements, requires strength, resilience, and corrosion resistance. High-tensile steel, known for its robustness, is the material of choice for withstanding the relentless forces of the ocean.

Yet, as a floating city, the ship's interior necessitates a delicate balance between luxury and practicality. Lightweight, fire-resistant materials are thoughtfully incorporated into passenger areas, ensuring safety without compromising comfort and elegance.

In harmonizing these contrasting material requirements, shipbuilders masterfully orchestrate a symphony of strength and efficiency, turning raw materials into a sophisticated vessel that stands resilient against the might of the seas.

Evolution of Cruise Ship Designs

Cruise ships have undergone tremendous transformation since the earliest days of ocean travel. This chapter will trace the evolution of cruise ship designs, highlighting how they have changed in response to technological advances, safety regulations, and passenger expectations.

We began with the steamship era of the late 19th century when ships like the SS Great Western and the SS Britannia represented the cutting edge of maritime design. These vessels featured basic passenger accommodations and were primarily used for transatlantic crossings.

The turn of the 20th century brought more luxurious and larger vessels like the RMS Titanic and the RMS Queen Mary. These "floating palaces" emphasized luxury and comfort, with lavish interiors, multiple dining options, and leisure facilities, setting the stage for the modern cruising concept.

Post World War II, the advent of transatlantic flights led to a decline in ocean liners. However, the industry adapted, and the focus shifted from transportation to vacationing, marking the birth of the "cruise ship." We explore this shift with examples like the SS Norway, converted from an ocean liner to a cruise ship, offering an array of amenities aimed at vacationers.

The late 20th century and early 21st century witnessed a trend toward more prominent and extravagant ships. We discuss the design aspects of these "mega ships," such as Royal Caribbean's Oasis Class and Norwegian Cruise Line's Breakaway Class, which carry thousands of passengers and offer unprecedented features such as onboard parks, shopping districts, and surf simulators.

As the cruise ship industry faces growing calls for sustainability, we also delve into the recent innovations in environmentally-friendly design and fuel efficiency. We examine the adoption of technologies such as liquefied natural gas (LNG) propulsion and advanced wastewater treatment systems.

Finally, we speculate on the future of cruise ship designs. Will they continue to get bigger? Or will the emphasis shift towards more sustainable, eco-friendly designs? How might technologies like AI and automation influence the future design of these vessels? This chapter offers an in-depth look at cruise ship design's past, present, and potential future.

Modern Cruise Ship Design Features and Amenities

In the contemporary era, cruise ship design goes beyond functional necessity. These cruise ships have become floating resorts with various amenities and attractions for all ages, tastes, and interests.

Cabins and Suites

The accommodations on a modern cruise ship are meticulously designed to offer comfort and luxury, regardless of the room's size or price point. From interior cabins, typically the smallest and most affordable, to multi-room suites with private balconies and ocean views, there is an option to suit every traveler's budget and preferences. Solo travelers can find specially designed single cabins. At the same time, large families or groups can enjoy spacious family suites equipped with multiple bedrooms and bathrooms.

Guests can expect hotel-like amenities inside these cabins and suites, including comfortable beds, private bathrooms, televisions, mini-fridges, and often a sitting area. Larger suites may include additional luxuries such as walk-in closets, whirlpool tubs, and private outdoor spaces. Cruise ship cabins are designed to maximize space and storage, with intelligent solutions like under-bed storage and versatile furniture.

Dining Options

Dining on a cruise ship is a culinary journey, with menus catering to various tastes and dietary requirements. Most ships offer a main dining room with a rotating menu, varied casual buffet and grill options, specialty restaurants, and round-the-clock room service.

The main dining rooms are grand spaces, often spanning two decks, designed to evoke the glamour of a bygone era of cruising. Casual dining venues are usually strategically located near the pool or central hub, offering a relaxed ambiance. Specialty restaurants range from steakhouses to sushi bars, Italian trattorias, and even chef's table experiences with menus curated by renowned chefs.

Designing these dining facilities involves careful space planning to accommodate a large number of guests while maintaining a comfortable dining experience. Kitchens are marvels of efficiency, designed to produce thousands of meals each day while meeting stringent hygiene standards.

Entertainment Venues

Entertainment venues on cruise ships are architectural feats, hosting everything from Broadway-style shows to live concerts. Large ships often have multi-tiered main theaters featuring state-of-the-art sound and lighting systems, enormous LED screens, and intricate stage mechanisms for ambitious performances.

Other entertainment venues include smaller lounges for live music and comedy acts, outdoor movie screens for under-the-stars cinema experiences, and multipurpose rooms for activities like dance classes and bingo. Some ships have even introduced high-tech entertainment options like virtual reality experiences and escape rooms.

Recreational Facilities

From swimming pools and hot tubs to water slides and splash zones, cruise ships offer a variety of water-based recreational facilities. Some ships feature multiple pool areas, each designed with a different ambiance - a lively main pool, a quieter adults-only pool, and a fun-filled family pool.

But it's not all about the water. Modern cruise ships boast impressive sports facilities, including fully-equipped gyms, jogging tracks, basketball courts, mini-golf courses, and even unique attractions like rock climbing walls, ropes courses, or surf simulators. These facilities are designed with safety in mind, ensuring guests stay active and entertained at sea.

Spa and Wellness Centers

Spa and wellness centers on cruise ships offer a tranquil retreat for passengers looking to relax and rejuvenate. These spaces are often designed with a serene and soothing aesthetic, utilizing elements of nature in their decor. Passengers can indulge in various treatments, from massages and facials to acupuncture and medi-spa services. Many cruise ship spas also include thermal suites featuring saunas, steam rooms, and heated loungers, and some offer thalassotherapy pools filled with mineral-rich seawater.

Shops and Retail Spaces

Cruise ship shopping ranges from logo apparel and convenience items to luxury jewelry and duty-free alcohol and tobacco. Shops are typically grouped in a central location, often designed to mimic a traditional mall or department store with window displays and carefully arranged merchandise.

These retail spaces are a significant revenue source for cruise lines, and their design and placement on the ship are strategic. The selection of goods also reflects the demographics of the ship's passengers and the regions the ship is traveling through.

Bars, Lounges, and Nightclubs

Cruise ships offer various nightlife options, each with a unique design and ambiance. Cocktail bars might provide a chic, sophisticated environment. In contrast, a pub or sports bar offers a casual, laid-back setting. Nightclubs on cruise ships are designed with soundproofing, lighting effects, and dance floors, offering a place for passengers to dance the night away.

Many ships also offer outdoor deck parties with live music and special events like themed nights or fireworks displays. The design of these spaces allows for flexibility, as they may be used for different purposes throughout the day.

Children and Teen Facilities

Younger cruisers are well catered for on modern cruise ships, with dedicated clubs and activity programs for different age groups. Children's areas include spaces for art and crafts, games, and even small playgrounds. At the same time, teen clubs feature video games, music, and a relaxed lounge area.

These facilities are designed with safety and fun, providing age-appropriate entertainment and the chance for young passengers to socialize with others their age. Many cruise lines also offer babysitting or late-night group childcare services, allowing parents to enjoy adult-only time on board.

Art Collections

Art is a prominent feature on many cruise ships, with some vessels showcasing collections worth millions of dollars. Passengers can enjoy a self-guided art tour, attend art auctions, or appreciate the carefully curated pieces that adorn public spaces.

The art on cruise ships often reflects the ship's overall design aesthetic or theme. It can range from paintings and sculptures to installations and multimedia works. This feature enhances the cultural experience onboard and promotes a sophisticated atmosphere.

Case Studies: Most Renowned Cruise Ships

Queen Mary 2 (Cunard Line)

Often referred to as the last true ocean liner, the Queen Mary 2 stands as a testament to the grandeur of transatlantic voyages of the past. Launched in 2004, she features a timeless design with modern touches. The QM2's unique amenities include the only planetarium at sea, a 1,094-seat theater, and one of the largest ballrooms afloat. The ship also distinguishes itself by providing kennels for passengers traveling with pets.

Symphony of the Seas (Royal Caribbean International)

Symphony of the Seas is the world's largest cruise ship. Launched in 2018, it represents the pinnacle of contemporary cruise ship design with features like a 10-story slide, two rock-climbing walls, a zipline, a surf simulator, and even an ice-skating rink. The ship's innovative "neighborhood" concept divides the enormous ship into seven distinct areas, including the tree-lined Central Park and the Boardwalk, which features a carousel and the AquaTheater for high-diving aquatic performances.

Disney Dream (Disney Cruise Line)

Disney Dream, launched in 2011, captures the magic of Disney in a ship. The interior design is reminiscent of classic 1930s ocean liners but with a generous sprinkling of Disney characters. Unique features include magical portholes for inside staterooms, which provide real-time views with occasional Disney character appearances, and the Aquaduck, the first water coaster at sea. The ship also offers Broadway-style Disney musicals, character meet-and-greets, and first-run Disney films, often in 3D.

MS Koningsdam (Holland America Line)

Launched in 2016, the Koningsdam is Holland America's largest ship and the first in their Pinnacle Class. The ship blends the line's history with modern touches and innovative features. The design is inspired by the "architecture of music," with fluid lines and spaces that flow like a symphony. Notable features include World Stage, a theater with a two-story, 270-degree wraparound LED screen, and Blend, where guests can blend their wine. The ship's Music Walk offers different live music venues, from classical to rock.

Celebrity Edge (Celebrity Cruises)

Celebrity Edge, launched in 2018, has a design that sets new standards in ship design. The ship features the innovative Magic Carpet, a movable deck that serves different functions, from a specialty restaurant to an extension of the pool area, depending on its position. Another unique feature is the Infinite Veranda staterooms, where with the touch of a button, guests can transform their room to incorporate the balcony area, providing more space and uninterrupted views. The ship also boasts Eden, a three-story venue changing from a skillful lounge during the day to an entertainment venue at night.

Each of these ships offers a unique cruising experience shaped by their design and the amenities they provide. Their success testifies to the crucial role of ship design in defining the cruise experience and setting a cruise line apart in a competitive industry.

3

The Economic Impact of Cruise Ships

Global Economic Footprint of the Cruise Ship Industry

The cruise ship industry is an influential player in the world economy, driving billions of dollars in economic activity annually. This economic footprint extends beyond mere profits generated from cruise packages. It encompasses employment in various sectors, procurement of goods and services, infrastructure development, and indirect contributions to the economies of port cities and regions.

Job Creation

The cruise industry supports millions of jobs globally, directly and indirectly. Direct employment includes crew members, administrative staff, and those in shipbuilding and maintenance. The cruise industry also stimulates indirect employment in local tourism sectors like restaurants, transport services, souvenir shops, etc.

Goods and Services Procurement

The cruise industry procures various goods and services, from fuel and food to professional services and shipbuilding materials. These purchases support economic activity across different sectors and often bolster small and medium-sized enterprises.

Infrastructure Enhancement

Port and tourism-related infrastructures often need to be developed or upgraded to accommodate larger vessels and an influx of tourists, indirectly fostering local construction activity.

Government Revenue

Cruise lines pay taxes and port fees, providing an additional revenue stream for local and national governments. This revenue often goes towards maintaining and enhancing port facilities and other infrastructure.

However, the economic benefits of the cruise ship industry need to be considered against the backdrop of potential environmental impacts and over-tourism risks. Achieving sustainable growth requires a balanced approach that mitigates adverse effects while leveraging the industry's economic potential.

The Role of Cruise Tourism in Local Economies

Cruise tourism is a vital component of many local economies, particularly in regions heavily reliant on tourism. The arrival of a cruise ship ushers in a host of tourists keen on local attractions, culinary experiences, and shopping, thereby infusing the local economy with a substantial boost.

Impact on Tourism and Retail

The arrival of a cruise ship has an immediate and significant effect on local tourism and retail sectors. Cruise passengers participate in shore excursions, visit cultural, historical, and natural attractions, and contribute substantially to the local retail industry through their expenditures.

Employment Stimulus

The demand surge associated with cruise tourism leads to job creation across tourism, hospitality, and retail sectors. This translates into direct employment opportunities such as tour operators, hospitality staff, and shopkeepers and indirect employment via increased demand for local goods and services.

Community Development

The revenue generated from cruise tourism often gets directed toward community development initiatives. This can result in improved public services, enhanced local facilities, and an overall improved quality of life for residents.

However, there are potential challenges associated with cruise tourism. The sudden surge of tourists can strain local resources and infrastructure, and the benefits might be unevenly distributed. Furthermore, an over-reliance on cruise tourism might expose local economies to the industry's volatility. Strategic tourism management practices are crucial to optimize the advantages of cruise tourism, ensuring a balance between economic gains and sustainable practices.

Case Study: Economic Benefits of Cruise Tourism in Popular Destinations

To understand the economic benefits of cruise tourism, let's examine popular destinations.

Caribbean Islands

The Caribbean Islands are among the most visited cruise destinations worldwide. The allure of crystal-clear waters, white sandy beaches, vibrant culture, and warm climate draws millions of cruise tourists annually.

Cruise tourism has been a significant economic driver for these island nations. With an influx of visitors, local businesses such as restaurants, shops, and tour companies thrive. It's estimated that cruise tourists spend an average of $100 per port visit, contributing millions to the local economy.

Alaska

Cruise tourism is also crucial to Alaska's economy. The state's breathtaking scenery, diverse wildlife, and unique cultural heritage attract thousands of cruise tourists annually.

Cruise tourism in Alaska supports thousands of jobs, primarily in the hospitality, retail, and tour sectors. The industry also generates substantial state revenue through head taxes, gaming taxes, and corporate income taxes from cruise lines. It's reported that cruise passengers in Alaska spend an average of $160 per port visit, considerably boosting the local economy.

Mediterranean Region

The Mediterranean's rich history, beautiful coastlines, and cultural diversity is another favorite cruise destination. The region sees a significant economic impact from cruise tourism. Tourists flock to historical cities such as Rome, Athens, and Barcelona, spending money on tours, local cuisine, and souvenirs. The influx of cruise passengers notably impacts local businesses and job creation. The Mediterranean region also benefits from the increased port activity, encouraging infrastructure development and modernization.

However, cities like Venice and Barcelona have also experienced the adverse effects of over-tourism, forcing local authorities to implement strategies for sustainable tourism to balance economic benefits with the preservation of their cultural heritage and environment.

Australia and New Zealand

Australia and New Zealand's unique ecosystems, vibrant cities, and cultural attractions make them popular destinations for cruise tourists. In Australia, the cruise industry contributes over a billion dollars to the national economy and supports thousands of jobs. Popular ports like Sydney, Melbourne, and Brisbane see significant spending from cruise passengers, boosting local businesses and the tourism industry.

In New Zealand, the cruise industry also plays an essential economic role, especially in port cities like Auckland, Wellington, and Dunedin. Cruise passengers often engage in shore excursions to explore local attractions, creating revenue for tour operators and other local businesses.

The cruise industry's presence in both countries drives infrastructure development, with port enhancements and transportation improvements to accommodate the increasing numbers of cruise tourists.

Asian Destinations

The Asia-Pacific region is emerging as a vibrant cruise market, with countries like Japan, China, and Singapore becoming popular cruise destinations. These countries benefit economically from cruise tourism through direct spending, job creation, and infrastructure development. In Singapore, the cruise industry supports the tourism sector. It stimulates business for the city's retail, dining, and entertainment industries.

However, as with other regions, the cruise industry's growth in Asia brings challenges, including environmental concerns and the pressure of over-tourism. These countries must manage cruise tourism growth sustainably to balance economic benefits with environmental and cultural preservation.

4

The Environmental Impact of Cruise Ships

Cruise ships are marvels of modern engineering, providing unforgettable experiences to millions of passengers each year. However, these floating cities have significant environmental implications beneath the glamour and fun. With the growing awareness of ecological sustainability, understanding the environmental impact of cruise ships has become a topic of paramount importance.

This chapter will delve into the different facets of the environmental implications of cruise ships, ranging from waste management issues to air and water pollution, fuel consumption, and noise and light pollution. It will shed light on international regulations and agreements that govern these impacts and highlight some of the initiatives taken by the cruise industry to minimize their environmental footprint.

The environmental impacts of cruise ships are a multifaceted issue requiring careful consideration. As the cruise industry continues to grow, balancing the need for economic development with environmental sustainability will be a vital challenge. By better understanding these impacts, stakeholders, including cruise operators, policymakers, passengers, and communities in destination ports, can make informed decisions contributing to a more sustainable future for cruise tourism.

Waste Management Issues and Impacts

Like floating cities, cruise ships generate substantial waste that needs proper management to prevent adverse environmental impacts. Among the most common waste streams are sewage, gray water, hazardous wastes, oily bilge water, ballast water, and solid waste.

Sewage and Grey Water

Cruise ships generate significant sewage and grey water from showers, sinks, laundries, and kitchens. The handling and discharge of these waste streams are critical environmental concerns. If not treated correctly before being discharged, they can introduce nutrients and pathogens into marine ecosystems, leading to water pollution, harm to aquatic life, and potential health risks to humans.

Hazardous Wastes

Cruise ships produce hazardous wastes such as batteries, fluorescent lights, medical wastes, and expired chemicals. Suppose these dangerous materials are not appropriately disposed of. In that case, they can seriously risk marine ecosystems and human health.

Oily Bilge Water

Bilgewater accumulates in the lower part of the ship and often contains oil, grease, and other contaminants. Before the remaining water can be discharged overboard, the oil must be treated on board to separate it. Failure to do so can result in oil pollution, causing significant harm to marine life and ecosystems.

Ballast Water

Ships take in ballast water for stability, but this water can contain various biological materials, including plants, animals, viruses, and bacteria, picked up from the original location. Suppose this ballast water is released in a new area. In that case, it can introduce invasive species that harm local ecosystems and biodiversity.

Solid Waste

Cruise ships generate a significant amount of solid waste like food waste, packaging, and other disposables. Incorrect disposal of solid waste can lead to marine pollution, impacting aquatic life and the overall health of our oceans.

Addressing these waste management challenges is vital for the cruise industry to minimize its environmental impact. Several international agreements, regulations, and industry practices guide waste management on cruise ships. Some cruise lines have also taken initiatives to implement advanced waste treatment systems, reduce waste generation, and increase recycling and reuse. Despite these measures, ongoing monitoring and improvements are necessary to ensure the industry's sustainability.

Air and Water Pollution Concerns

While waste management is a significant concern in the operation of cruise ships, it's also essential to address the issues of air and water pollution. Given their massive size and the duration of their voyages, cruise ships have substantial fuel needs, leading to significant air emissions. Simultaneously, the various onboard activities also contribute to potential water pollution.

Air Pollution

Cruise ships, much like any large transportation vessel, emit air pollutants, including carbon dioxide (CO_2), nitrogen oxides (NOx), and sulfur oxides (SOx), due to the combustion of marine diesel oil or heavy fuel oil in their engines. In particular, the high sulfur content of rich fuel oil many cruise lines use results in higher sulfur dioxide emissions than other transportation forms. These emissions contribute to global climate change, harm human health, and negatively impact air quality, particularly in port cities where the ships often idle with engines running to provide power to onboard services.

Increasingly, the cruise industry has been exploring cleaner fuels like liquefied natural gas (LNG) and investing in technologies such as exhaust gas cleaning systems, commonly known as "scrubbers," which reduce the sulfur content of the exhaust gases. Yet, these solutions have their own challenges and controversies.

Fuel Use and Implications for Greenhouse Gas Emissions

Cruise ships primarily use marine gas oil (MGO) and heavy fuel oil (HFO) like other large vessels. While MGO is cleaner-burning, HFO, derived from crude oil, is used more frequently due to its cost-effectiveness. However, it's important to note that the combustion of HFO results in higher emissions of greenhouse gases (GHGs), particularly carbon dioxide (CO_2), contributing significantly to global climate change.

Cruise ships can consume massive volumes of fuel daily, depending on their size, speed, and number of onboard amenities. This high fuel consumption equates to substantial CO_2 emissions. The International Council on Clean Transportation reported in 2019 that the cruise ship industry released more than 21 million tons of CO_2 in 2017 alone.

Moreover, due to their vast size and the considerable power needed for their operation, cruise ships have a higher CO_2 emission per passenger per kilometer than most other transport modes. This high emission intensity and the cruise industry's growing popularity pose a significant challenge to global efforts to reduce GHG emissions and combat climate change.

The cruise industry, acknowledging its role in climate change, has begun taking steps to curb its emissions. There's a growing interest in alternative, cleaner fuels, such as liquefied natural gas (LNG), biofuels, and even the possibility of hybrid electric ships. Several cruise lines have ordered LNG-powered ships, significantly reducing CO_2, SO_x, and NO_x emissions.

Nevertheless, switching to alternative fuels is challenging. For instance, the infrastructure for supplying LNG in ports worldwide has yet to fully develop. Similarly, while electric propulsion can be a sustainable option, it poses significant technical and economic challenges for large cruise ships.

Furthermore, energy-efficient technologies and practices have been adopted, such as advanced hull designs, air lubrication systems, heat recovery systems, and energy management systems. Some cruise lines also explore shore power - connecting to local electrical grids while in port to avoid running their engines and thus reduce emissions.

While these initiatives are promising, effectively mitigating the cruise industry's climate impact requires technical solutions, policy interventions, industry commitment, and increased awareness among cruise passengers. Navigating towards a more sustainable cruise industry will be a journey in itself.

Regulatory Measures and Agreements: MARPOL IV-14 and Beyond

Various international regulations and agreements have been instituted to mitigate the impact in response to the environmental concerns of the shipping industry, including cruise ships. Among these, one of the most notable is the International Convention for the Prevention of Pollution from Ships, or

MARPOL.

MARPOL is a set of international regulations designed to minimize marine pollution from ships. It includes six technical annexes that address different types of ship-borne pollution – oil, noxious liquid substances, harmful substances in packaged form, sewage, garbage, and air pollution.

Annex VI, the latest addition, targets air pollution from ships, including sulfur oxides (SOx), nitrogen oxides (NOx), and greenhouse gases. Regulation 14 under this Annex, known as MARPOL IV-14, focuses explicitly on sulfur emissions. It mandates that the sulfur content of fuel oil used on board ships should not exceed 0.50% m/m (mass by mass) globally from 1 January 2020, a significant reduction from the previous limit of 3.50% m/m.

The limit is even stricter in designated Emission Control Areas (ECAs) at 0.10% m/m. Alternatively, ships can meet the SOx emission requirements by using exhaust gas cleaning systems, or "scrubbers," which clean the emissions before they are released into the atmosphere.

While MARPOL IV-14 is a crucial step toward reducing the environmental impact of cruise ships, its effectiveness relies heavily on enforcement. Monitoring and enforcing compliance with emission standards on the high seas is a considerable challenge. It requires international cooperation, stringent oversight, and significant resources.

Furthermore, while Annex VI addresses greenhouse gas emissions from ships, it does not yet include specific reduction targets or measures. In light of the Paris Agreement's goals and the urgent need to reduce global GHG emissions, the International Maritime Organization (IMO) is developing a strategy to reduce GHGs from ships. The scheme envisages, among other things, reducing carbon intensity from shipping – the carbon emissions per transport work – by at least 40% by 2030 and halving total annual GHG emissions from shipping by 2050 compared to 2008.

In addition to international regulations, various voluntary schemes and initiatives aim to improve the environmental performance of cruise ships. These include certification schemes like Green Award and Blue Flag, which recognize ships demonstrating superior environmental performance.

While substantial progress has been made in regulating pollution from cruise ships, more stringent regulations, better enforcement, and more significant industry commitment are needed to ensure a sustainable future for the cruise industry.

Case Studies: Cruise Lines Taking Steps to Reduce Environmental Impact

The cruise industry's environmental impact has led many companies to take proactive steps toward mitigating their ecological footprint. Here, we'll take a closer look at several cruise lines that are making strides in this area, presenting new standards for the industry.

Royal Caribbean's Advanced Emission Purification (AEP)

Systems

Royal Caribbean has equipped many of its ships with Advanced Emission Purification (AEP) systems, also known as scrubbers. These systems remove up to 98% of the sulfur dioxide emissions generated by the ship's engines, significantly reducing the impact of these vessels on air quality. In addition to the AEP systems, Royal Caribbean has committed to a 35% reduction in its carbon footprint by 2030, a goal it is pursuing through various energy efficiency and fuel-saving measures.

Hurtigruten's Hybrid Expedition Ships

Norwegian cruise line Hurtigruten has been at the forefront of environmental innovation in the industry. The company launched the world's first hybrid electric-powered expedition ship, the MS Roald Amundsen, in 2019. This groundbreaking vessel uses large battery packs to support its low-emission engines, reducing CO_2 emissions by more than 20% compared to ships of a similar size. The company is also converting several of its existing ships to run on biogas, LNG, and large battery packs, pushing the envelope for what's possible in green ship technology.

MSC Cruises' Investment in LNG-Powered Ships

MSC Cruises, one of the largest cruise companies globally, has shown a solid commitment to sustainable operations. The company has invested significantly in liquified natural gas (LNG) technology, currently the cleanest fossil fuel available for marine operations. In 2022, MSC launched the MSC World

Europa, the first in a new class of LNG-powered cruise ships. It's part of the company's plan to have at least nine LNG-powered cruise ships in service by 2027. MSC is also exploring cutting-edge technologies like solid oxide fuel cells, which offer the prospect of zero-emission operations.

Carnival Corporation's Cold Ironing Initiatives

Carnival Corporation, the world's largest leisure travel company, has implemented cold ironing capabilities across its fleet. Cold ironing, also known as shore power, allows a ship to shut off its engines and plug into an electrical grid while docked, significantly reducing emissions in port cities. As of 2023, 43% of Carnival's fleet is equipped with cold ironing technology, and the company has committed to increasing this percentage in the future.

These case studies illustrate that the cruise industry increasingly recognizes the importance of reducing its environmental impact and finding innovative ways to achieve this goal. It also underlines the need for a concerted industry-wide effort to perform more sustainable operations.

5

Cruise Ships and Overtourism

Definition and Causes of Overtourism

Overtourism, as its name implies, refers to a situation with too many visitors to a particular destination. When tourism activity is within the capacity of a location to handle it, the result is often an undesirable impact on the environment, infrastructure, and local quality of life. While it can generate economic prosperity, over-tourism can also create significant challenges, leading to strain on natural resources, degradation of landmarks, increased pollution, and disturbance to local communities.

Cruise ships can significantly contribute to over-tourism, particularly in popular port cities and island destinations. Several factors are at play.

Large Volume of Visitors

A modern cruise ship can carry thousands of passengers, and

when a ship docks, it can dramatically increase the population of a locality within a short period. This sudden influx can overwhelm local facilities and infrastructure, particularly in smaller or less developed destinations.

Short, Intense Visits

Cruise ship passengers typically spend a few hours to a day at a port of call. This results in a concentration of tourist activity within short periods, which can increase crowding and put pressure on attractions, services, and resources.

Seasonality

Cruise ship visits are often seasonal, leading to periods of extreme visitor concentration followed by periods with few visitors. This pattern can make it challenging for destinations to manage resources and infrastructure effectively.

Limited Local Economic Benefits

While cruise tourism can contribute to local economies, there are concerns that a significant portion of the economic benefits should be retained locally. Many cruise passengers eat and shop onboard the ship. The cruise lines often organize shore excursions, limiting the interaction and direct spending with local businesses.

Lack of Local Control

Cruise ship visits and passenger activities are primarily controlled by the cruise companies, not the local authorities or communities. This can limit the ability of destinations to manage tourism in a way that best serves their interests.

Addressing the issue of over-tourism requires a concerted effort from all stakeholders, including cruise companies, local authorities, and communities. Strategies include managing visitor numbers, improving tourist behavior, diversifying tourist activities, and ensuring that the economic benefits of tourism are equitably distributed. This complex issue is further explored in the following sections of this book.

Cruise Ships' Role in Overtourism

Cruise ships have revolutionized the way people travel and enjoy their vacations. Their immense size and capacity to carry thousands of passengers to exotic locations worldwide have made them a popular choice for holidaymakers. However, their increasing popularity and size have inadvertently positioned them as significant contributors to the over-tourism phenomenon in some locales.

Impact on Local Communities and Infrastructure

When thousands of passengers disembark from a cruise ship and explore a port city en masse, the sudden surge of tourists can disrupt daily life for local residents and strain existing infrastructures, such as roads, public transportation, and utilities. For instance, the historic waterways of Venice, Italy, have felt the pressure of accommodating large cruise vessels, leading to calls for limitations on their access.

Heritage Site Deterioration

High traffic levels at historical and cultural sites due to cruise ship passengers can lead to accelerated deterioration of these places. The enormous visitor footfall often surpasses the site's capacity, leading to congestion, damage to structures, and potential loss of cultural integrity.

Environmental Strain

The visit of cruise ships can also put stress on local ecosystems. For example, marine environments can be adversely impacted by anchoring ships. At the same time, terrestrial ecosystems may struggle with increased litter or habitat disturbances from high numbers of visitors.

Shaping Tourist Expectations and Behaviors

Cruise ship tourism often promotes a particular type of consumption-oriented tourism, emphasizing sightseeing, shopping, and dining experiences. This type of tourism can sometimes overshadow other forms of engagement with the destination, such as learning about local cultures or contributing to sustainable practices.

Cruise ships' role in over-tourism highlights the need for better management of cruise ship tourism. This includes improved planning and coordination between cruise companies and destination communities, regulations to limit the size and number of ships in sensitive locations, and efforts to encourage more sustainable tourist behaviors. Solutions must be multifaceted, balancing the tourism sector's economic benefits with preserving the charm and integrity of destinations.

Venice

Venice, the Italian city famed for its canals and gondolas, is one of the most potent examples of over-tourism exacerbated by cruise ships. Before restrictions were imposed due to over-tourism, this city of just over 50,000 residents would witness cruise ships delivering up to 30,000 visitors daily during peak season. The large ships, towering over the city's skyline, have been accused of contributing to erosion, water pollution, and damaging the foundations of historic buildings. Due to public outcry and growing environmental concerns, the Italian government recently decided to divert large cruise ships away from the city's historic center, rerouting them to less fragile areas.

Barcelona

Barcelona, Spain's second-largest city, is another destination grappling with the effects of overtourism. As one of Europe's top cruise ship destinations, the city receives millions of passengers yearly, significantly adding to its visitor numbers. The massive influx of tourists from cruise ships and other forms of tourism has led to local protests and calls for better tourism management. In response, the city's authorities have imposed regulations to limit the number of tourist accommodations and initiated discussions about capping the number of cruise ships allowed to dock.

Dubrovnik

Dubrovnik, known as the 'Pearl of the Adriatic,' became a hot spot for tourists, particularly after featuring in the hit series "Game of Thrones." Many tourists, many arriving on cruise ships, have threatened the city's cultural heritage, including its UNESCO World Heritage Site status. The city's medieval walls and narrow streets were not designed to cope with the thousands of tourists arriving daily. Apologies for that oversight. In response to the issue, the city introduced a 'Respect the City' plan, which implements measures such as limiting the number of cruise ship passengers allowed to disembark each day and restricting the number of cruise ships that can dock simultaneously. The city has also started monitoring real-time visitor numbers to better manage the flow of tourists.

Cruise Ship Scheduling and Limitations

Several tourist destinations are revisiting their cruise ship docking schedules and imposing limits on the number of ships that can dock daily. They aim to distribute the number of visitors more evenly throughout the year and limit the number of tourists present at any given time. This approach seeks to alleviate the pressure on local resources and infrastructure while reaping tourism's economic benefits.

Visitor Caps

Certain cities, like Dubrovnik and Bar Harbor, Maine, impose daily caps on the number of cruise ship passengers allowed to disembark. These caps are part of a broader strategy to manage tourist numbers and protect local communities and environments. It also ensures that the influx of visitors remains within the city's capacity to work effectively.

Alternative Routing

In cases where the docking of cruise ships directly impacts sensitive environments, such as in Venice, alternative routing has been introduced. This approach entails rerouting cruise ships from vulnerable areas, minimizing potential environmental damage.

Promoting Off-Peak Travel

Encouraging cruise ships to visit in the off-peak season can also be an effective strategy to mitigate over-tourism. This reduces pressure during peak seasons and helps spread the economic benefits of tourism more evenly throughout the year.

Encouraging Sustainable Practices

Some port cities are working with cruise lines to encourage sustainable tourism practices. This might include developing onshore power capabilities to allow docked ships to reduce emissions, promoting local and sustainable shore excursions, or encouraging tourists to respect local cultures and environments.

Implementing Tourist Taxes

Several destinations are also introducing or increasing tourist taxes for cruise ship passengers. This additional revenue can offset the costs associated with over-tourism, such as maintaining and upgrading infrastructure, protecting local environments, or investing in local communities. It also can serve to deter excessive numbers of tourists.

However, while these measures can help to mitigate the impact of cruise ship-related over-tourism, they are not a panacea. More holistic and coordinated efforts are needed globally to ensure cruise tourism's sustainable development.

6

Maritime Safety and Cruise Ships

Despite being floating cities, cruise ships have stringent safety measures and regulations to ensure the well-being of all onboard. These safety protocols encompass various aspects of maritime safety, from navigation to fire safety, medical emergencies, and more. Here, we discuss some essential safety measures and regulations governing cruise ship operations.

Navigation Safety

Navigating a massive cruise ship through the open seas and into ports requires high expertise. Cruise ships have state-of-the-art navigational tools like GPS, radar, and electronic chart display systems to ensure safe navigation. They also follow strict routing measures under the guidance of trained maritime officers. In addition, when entering or leaving port, local pilots with specialized knowledge of the waterways are often brought on board to guide the ship.

Fire Safety

Fire safety is critical to cruise ship safety. Ships are designed with multiple fire zones to prevent the spread of fire. They are equipped with advanced fire detection and suppression systems. In addition, strict safety regulations require regular fire drills for crew members and clearly marked evacuation routes for passengers.

Life-Saving Equipment

Cruise ships must carry enough life-saving equipment, including life jackets and lifeboats, for everyone onboard. Regular drills ensure crew and passengers know how to use this equipment in an emergency.

Medical Facilities

Most cruise ships have onboard medical facilities to handle various health issues. These medical centers are often staffed by trained medical professionals capable of addressing everything from minor ailments to more severe conditions. They can even perform minor surgeries if needed.

Security Measures

Cruise ships have strict security measures in place to ensure passenger safety. These include controlled access points, security personnel, and surveillance systems. In addition, the International Ship and Port Facility Security (ISPS) Code, an amendment to the Safety of Life at Sea (SOLAS) Convention, sets mandatory security procedures for ships and port facilities to deter security threats.

Sanitation Standards

Sanitation is a crucial aspect of safety on cruise ships. In the US, cruise ships are subject to unannounced inspections by the Vessel Sanitation Program (VSP) of the Centers for Disease Control and Prevention (CDC) to ensure they meet stringent health and sanitation standards.

Each of these safety measures and regulations plays a vital role in ensuring the safety of passengers and crew members alike. They underscore the cruise industry's commitment to maintaining a safe and healthy environment onboard its vessels.

Health and Safety Issues: From Sea Sickness to Pandemics

Health and safety issues on cruise ships encompass a broad spectrum, from common disorders such as seasickness to more significant concerns, including disease outbreaks. While cruise ships have measures to deal with these challenges, passengers must understand these issues and ways to mitigate them.

Seasickness

Seasickness, a form of motion sickness, is a common concern for many cruise ship passengers. The constant motion of a ship can disrupt one's sense of balance, leading to symptoms such as nausea, dizziness, and occasionally vomiting. Cruise ships' size and stabilizing technology minimize much of the motion felt on smaller boats. However, some passengers may still experience seasickness, particularly during rough seas. Over-the-counter medications, wristbands, and specific dietary approaches can help mitigate these symptoms. It's also often advised to book cabins in the ship's middle, where motion is typically less pronounced.

Disease Outbreaks

Disease outbreaks, particularly those of gastrointestinal illnesses such as norovirus, have made headlines in the cruise industry. Cruise ships' close quarters and communal nature can facilitate the spread of such diseases. In response, cruise lines have stringent sanitation practices, including deep-cleaning protocols and hand sanitizer stations throughout the ship.

However, these preventive measures were put to the test with the onset of the COVID-19 pandemic. The enclosed environment of a cruise ship posed a unique challenge, leading to significant outbreaks on several ships. In response, the industry introduced rigorous testing protocols, vaccination requirements for passengers and crew, mask mandates, social distancing measures, and enhanced onboard medical capabilities. Despite these efforts, the potential risk of disease outbreaks remains a significant health concern in cruising.

Medical Emergencies

Medical emergencies, such as heart attacks, strokes, or injuries, can occur on cruise ships anywhere. While most ships are equipped with medical centers that can handle various conditions, the level of care may differ from what's available in a land-based hospital. For more severe conditions, evacuation to a shore-based facility may be necessary, which can be challenging depending on the ship's location.

Food and Water Safety

Foodborne illnesses and water safety are other potential health concerns. While cruise ships typically have strict food handling and water treatment procedures in place, instances of food poisoning can still occur.

Safety During Excursions

Health and safety risks also extend to shore excursions, where passengers must be aware of potential hazards, from sunburn and heatstroke in tropical climates to accidents during adventure activities.

In essence, while cruising offers a unique and enjoyable vacation option, it has potential health and safety issues. However, awareness of these concerns and appropriate preventive measures can significantly contribute to a safe and healthy cruise experience.

Case studies: Notable safety incidents and their outcomes

While most cruise ship voyages proceed without incident, a few notable safety-related cases have served as critical learning experiences for the industry. Below are brief overviews of three such instances.

Costa Concordia (2012)

The Costa Concordia disaster is one of the most infamous cruise ship incidents. The Italian cruise ship ran aground and capsized off the coast of Isola del Giglio, resulting in 32 deaths. The ship's captain, Francesco Schettino, was found guilty of manslaughter, causing a shipwreck, and abandoning the ship before all passengers were evacuated. This incident highlighted the importance of stringent safety protocols and training, leading to a renewed focus on safety drills and crew preparedness across the industry.

Diamond Princess (2020)

In early 2020, the Diamond Princess cruise ship became a significant news story as one of the earliest and most severe outbreaks of COVID-19 outside China. The ship was quarantined in Yokohama, Japan, with over 3,700 passengers and crew onboard. Over 700 people tested positive for the virus, and 14 died. This incident underscored the challenges of handling a highly infectious disease on a cruise ship. It prompted the industry to establish rigorous health protocols, including enhanced sanitation measures, social distancing guidelines, and testing requirements.

Viking Sky (2019)

In March 2019, the Viking Sky cruise ship suffered engine failure amid stormy weather off the coast of Norway. The vessel issued a mayday call as it drifted towards the rocky shore. A complex evacuation operation was conducted, airlifting more than 400 of the 1,300 passengers and crew before the crew restarted one engine and anchored the ship. While injuries were reported, there were no fatalities. This incident led to investigations and discussions about the safety of cruise ships and the necessity for effective emergency response plans.

These case studies represent significant challenges that the cruise industry has faced. In each instance, lessons learned have improved safety protocols, emergency preparedness, and disease prevention measures. Despite these incidents, cruising remains a popular vacation choice, and the industry continues to innovate and enhance its safety measures to ensure passenger well-being.

7

Sunken Vessels: A Historical Perspective

The Role of Human Error and Natural Disasters in Shipwrecks

Shipwrecks have a long and storied history, dating back to the earliest days of sea travel. While technology and safety measures have vastly improved over the centuries, every vessel is only partially impervious to mishaps. Both human error and natural disasters continue to play significant roles in shipwrecks.

Human Error

In many instances, human error has been a significant factor in shipwrecks. Such errors can occur at any level of a ship's operation, from the decisions of the captain and officers to the actions of individual crew members. These mistakes include navigation errors, improper ship equipment handling, inadequate maintenance, and failure to follow safety protocols.

For instance, the sinking of the RMS Titanic in 1912 is a notable case where human error played a decisive role. Despite warnings of icebergs in the area, the ship continued at high speed, leading to the fatal collision. Similarly, the Costa Concordia disaster in 2012 resulted primarily from the captain's decision to deviate from the planned route, causing the ship to hit a reef.

Natural Disasters

Natural disasters like hurricanes, typhoons, and rogue waves can also cause shipwrecks. Ships caught in severe storms can capsize, run aground, or suffer critical damage. Despite sophisticated weather forecasting systems and navigational aids, nature's unpredictability can still catch even the most experienced sailors off guard.

The sinking of the SS El Faro in 2015 exemplifies the potential danger of natural disasters. En route from Florida to Puerto Rico, the cargo ship was caught in Hurricane Joaquin. It sank, resulting in the loss of all 33 crew members. An investigation found that while the captain had been aware of the approaching hurricane, he had underestimated its intensity and path.

Both human error and natural disasters underscore the critical importance of continual learning, stringent safety measures, proper crew training, and respect for the power of nature in maritime operations. Each incident provides valuable lessons, leading to the development of better practices, safety protocols, and technologies to prevent future disasters.

Case Studies: Oceanos, Achille Lauro, Sea Diamond, Explorer, and Hableány

In exploring the history of sunken vessels, several cases stand out. These examples provide valuable insight into the factors that can contribute to maritime disasters, including severe weather, human error, and other unforeseen circumstances.

Oceanos

The sinking of the Oceanos cruise ship off the coast of South Africa in 1991 serves as a sobering reminder of the importance of crew professionalism and integrity. When the vessel began taking on water due to a burst pipe in the engine room, the crew reportedly abandoned the ship without raising the alarm, leaving passengers to fend for themselves. Thanks to the efforts of the onboard entertainers and a few brave passengers who managed to broadcast a distress signal, all 571 people onboard were eventually rescued by helicopters.

Achille Lauro

Initially launched in 1947, the Achille Lauro had a troubled history, culminating in its sinking in 1994. After catching fire off the coast of Somalia, the ship was abandoned and left to sink. This followed a notorious hijacking incident in 1985 when members of the Palestine Liberation Front took control of the vessel. All passengers and crew members were evacuated safely during the 1994 sinking. Still, the incident ended the vessel's turbulent history on the seas.

Sea Diamond

The Sea Diamond was a Greek cruise ship that sank in the Aegean

Sea in 2007, causing two fatalities. The boat hit a reef near the island of Santorini. It began taking on water, leading to the evacuation of the passengers and crew. The Sea Diamond eventually sank, causing a significant marine pollution incident.

Explorer

The Explorer was a cruise ship built for navigating polar regions. In 2007, the vessel hit an iceberg in the Antarctic and began to take on water. Although the ship ultimately sank, the crew evacuated all passengers safely. The incident highlighted the potential dangers of cruising in polar regions, even in modern, specially designed ships.

Hableány

The Hableány was a Hungarian river cruise ship that sank in the Danube River in Budapest in 2019 after being struck by a larger vessel. The incident led to losing 28 lives, mainly South Korean tourists. The collision and subsequent sinking raised issues about the traffic on the busy river. They sparked discussions on improved regulations for cruise ships' operations.

Each case study adds to the understanding of maritime safety, providing lessons for future improvements and emphasizing the critical need for comprehensive safety measures, efficient evacuation plans, and stringent regulations. They also serve as solemn reminders of the risks associated with sea travel and the importance of continually enhancing safety standards.

Lessons Learned and Safety Improvements After Each

Incident

After each maritime incident, thorough investigations are conducted to determine the causes and learn how similar disasters can be prevented in the future. Here, we delve into some of the lessons learned and safety improvements implemented following the notable incidents discussed earlier:

Oceanos

The Oceanos sinking exposed severe flaws in the crew's training and conduct. The incident was a stark reminder of the importance of maintaining a well-trained and professional crew, which must be prepared to prioritize passenger safety in emergencies. The Oceanos disaster also highlighted the significance of having clear evacuation procedures in place and regularly rehearsing these procedures with both crew and passengers.

Achille Lauro

The Achille Lauro incident reiterated the importance of having robust fire safety measures on cruise ships. The fire that led to the ship's sinking demonstrated the need for improved fire detection and suppression systems. After the incident, more stringent regulations were implemented, requiring better fire safety measures, including automatic sprinkler systems and fire detection devices in all passenger cabins and public areas.

Sea Diamond

The sinking of the Sea Diamond highlighted the need for better navigational systems and local knowledge to avoid hazards. As a result, greater emphasis has been placed on the importance of accurate marine charts, advanced electronic navigational tools, and the use of local pilots familiar with the region's specific challenges. The incident also underscored the critical role of immediate and efficient emergency evacuation procedures.

Explorer

The sinking of the Explorer in the Antarctic emphasized the unique dangers of polar cruising. It led to a thorough review of safety measures and regulations for ships operating in polar waters. In the years following the disaster, the International Maritime Organization introduced the Polar Code, which sets out mandatory safety and environmental standards for ships operating in these inhospitable waters.

Hableány

The Hableány tragedy sparked discussions on traffic regulations on busy rivers like the Danube. The incident emphasized the importance of traffic management, including effective communication and coordination between vessels, especially in high-traffic areas. In the aftermath, the authorities took steps to tighten navigation rules, and there has been an increased push for more advanced collision avoidance technology.

Each maritime disaster leaves behind critical lessons that help improve cruise ships' safety standards and procedures. Continued technological advancements, stricter regulations, and lessons from past incidents all play a crucial role in enhancing maritime safety, ensuring that the joy of cruising is not overshadowed by safety concerns.

8

The Future of Cruise Ships

Technological Innovations in Cruise Ship Design

Cruise ships continuously adapt to new technologies and innovations in a rapidly evolving world. Technological advancements aim to enhance passenger comfort and convenience and improve the industry's environmental footprint and safety measures. Here's a look at some emerging technological innovations in cruise ship design.

Advanced Energy Efficiency Technologies

In the face of increasing environmental regulations and public demand for sustainability, the cruise industry is exploring various technologies to enhance energy efficiency. For instance, new hull designs are being developed to reduce water resistance, while energy-efficient lighting and appliances are becoming standard. More sophisticated energy management systems are also employed to minimize onboard power usage.

LNG Powered Ships

Liquid Natural Gas (LNG) is becoming a cleaner alternative to traditional maritime fuels. Several cruise lines are already developing or operating ships powered by LNG, which significantly reduces air pollutants and helps the industry meet stringent emission standards.

Waste Heat Recovery

Another innovative technology is waste heat recovery, which involves capturing heat produced by the ship's engines and using it to generate electricity. This not only reduces energy consumption but also cuts down on greenhouse gas emissions.

Digital Connectivity

High-speed internet and digital technologies are becoming a fundamental cruise experience. Cruise lines invest in satellite and broadband technologies to provide onboard reliable, high-speed internet access. Additionally, using digital applications to manage bookings, facilitate onboard purchases, and navigate the ship is increasingly prevalent.

Autonomous Ships

While fully autonomous ships may still be some years away, the technology is advancing rapidly. The potential benefits include increased safety by eliminating human error and cost savings from reduced crew requirements.

Augmented and Virtual Reality

Augmented reality (AR) and virtual reality (VR) technologies are increasingly used to enhance passenger experiences. From virtual tours of the ship and ports of call to interactive games and entertainment, these technologies offer a wealth of possibilities for passenger engagement.

Smart Cabin Technology

Like smart homes, smart cabins are becoming a reality on cruise ships. Features may include voice-activated controls, facial recognition technology for personalized service, and advanced environmental controls to adjust lighting, temperature, and humidity based on passenger preferences.

The future of cruise ships looks bright with the advent of these technological innovations. These advancements aim to enhance the passenger experience and address critical industry challenges related to environmental sustainability and safety. As technology evolves, the cruise industry is set to become even more immersive, efficient, and sustainable.

Sustainability and Eco-Friendly Trends in Cruise Ship Operations

As the cruise ship industry evolves, it's increasingly focusing on sustainability and eco-friendly operations to minimize its environmental impact. The industry recognizes that maintaining the health of the oceans and destinations they visit is integral to their long-term success. Consequently, numerous trends emerge as the industry strives to become more eco-conscious.

Eco-Friendly Fuels

Beyond LNG, cruise lines are exploring other sustainable fuel options, including biofuels and hydrogen fuel cells. Biofuels, derived from organic materials such as vegetable oils and animal fats, have the potential to significantly reduce CO_2 emissions. Meanwhile, hydrogen fuel cells produce only water as a byproduct, making them an attractive, albeit technically challenging, option for the future.

Solar Power

Cruise lines are beginning to incorporate solar panels into their ship designs. Although solar power can't entirely replace conventional fuels due to the massive energy demands of cruise ships, it can supplement onboard power sources and reduce overall emissions.

Shore Power Technology

This technology allows ships to turn off their engines and connect to local electrical grids when docked, reducing air pollution in port cities. More cruise lines are installing shore power technology, and more ports are offering it as an option.

Advanced Wastewater Treatment Systems

Cruise lines install advanced wastewater treatment systems on their ships to treat, purify, and disinfect wastewater before discharging it into the ocean, going above and beyond regulatory requirements to protect marine ecosystems.

Sustainable Onboard Practices

From banning single-use plastics to implementing extensive recycling programs, cruise lines are adopting more sustainable practices onboard their ships. Many also source sustainable seafood, promote local and fair trade products, and reduce food waste through careful planning and donation programs.

Conservation Partnerships

Cruise lines are increasingly partnering with conservation organizations to support environmental initiatives and engage in responsible tourism practices. These partnerships involve various activities, from funding marine research and conservation projects to educating passengers about responsible tourism and environmental stewardship.

Sustainability and eco-friendliness are becoming central to cruise ship operations. With these trends gaining momentum, the cruise industry is showing its commitment to environmental responsibility and preserving the pristine environments that make cruising a unique and enjoyable experience. This evolution will likely continue as new technologies, practices, and partnerships offer further opportunities for eco-friendly operations.

Future Challenges and Opportunities for the Cruise Ship Industry

Challenges

Environmental Regulations

The tightening of environmental regulations is a significant challenge for the industry. Adhering to these regulations often involves substantial investments in new technology and infrastructure, such as scrubbers, LNG-powered ships, and shore power facilities. The industry must find ways to meet these regulations while remaining profitable.

Climate Change

Climate change poses multiple challenges, from rising sea levels affecting port facilities to more frequent and severe storms disrupting cruise itineraries. Moreover, as public awareness of climate change grows, cruise lines may face increased consumer scrutiny and demand for sustainable practices.

Overcrowding and Overtourism

Managing the impact of cruise tourism on local communities and environments will be a critical challenge. Cruise lines will need to collaborate with destinations to prevent overcrowding, protect local ecosystems, and ensure that the benefits of tourism are distributed equitably.

Health and Safety

Ensuring the health and safety of passengers and crew will remain a primary concern, especially in light of recent health crises. The industry must continually review and update its health and safety protocols to keep up with evolving threats.

Opportunities

Technological Innovation

Advances in technology present exciting opportunities for the cruise industry, from more energy-efficient ship designs to onboard digital innovations that enhance the passenger experience. Adopting new technologies can also help the industry overcome some of its challenges, particularly in environmental sustainability and health and safety.

Sustainable Tourism

There's a growing demand for sustainable and responsible travel experiences among consumers. Cruise lines that offer such experiences, whether through eco-friendly practices, cultural sensitivity, or partnerships with local communities, will likely attract these conscientious travelers.

Emerging Markets

As the middle class grows in countries like China and India, so does the potential market for cruise tourism. Developing customized offerings for these new markets could be a significant growth opportunity for the industry.

Expedition Cruising

There's increasing interest in expedition cruises to remote and pristine destinations, such as Antarctica and the Galapagos Islands. These cruises appeal to travelers seeking unique experiences. They can command higher prices, making them a lucrative niche for the industry.

Personalization

With data analytics and AI, cruise lines can offer passengers more personalized experiences. This could include customized itineraries, onboard activities, and dining options, enhancing passenger satisfaction and loyalty.

As the cruise ship industry sails into the future, it will undoubtedly face waves of both challenges and opportunities. It's an exciting time for the industry as it navigates these waters and shapes the future of cruise travel.

9

Conclusion

Cruise ships have come a long way since their origins as humble passenger vessels. They've grown into floating cities, and engineering marvels that offer a dizzying array of amenities and experiences. They play a significant role in the global economy, contributing billions of dollars and supporting millions of jobs. However, they also pose environmental challenges, from waste disposal to air and water pollution, and their role in over-tourism has raised concerns in many popular destinations.

At the same time, the industry has shown its capacity for innovation and change. From implementing new waste management systems and emissions reduction technologies to designing more energy-efficient ships, cruise lines are taking steps to reduce their environmental impact. The industry also has the potential to lead the way in sustainable tourism, offering experiences that respect local cultures, protect the environment, and contribute to local economies.

CONCLUSION

Closing Thoughts on the Impact and Future of Cruise Ships

As we disembark from this exploration of the world of cruise ships, it's worth pausing to marvel at these incredible vessels and the complex industry surrounding them. They represent human ingenuity and our innate desire to explore and connect with the world.

Cruise ships have shaped how we travel and have a powerful impact on the places we touch, both for better and worse. The challenges they present are significant, but they're not insurmountable. With innovation, cooperation, and a commitment to sustainability, the cruise industry has the potential to chart a course toward a future where cruise travel is an even more enriching and responsible way to see the world.

Ultimately, the story of cruise ships is about more than the ships themselves. It's a story about our relationship with the world and each other. As we sail into the future, let's aim to steer this story toward one of respect, responsibility, and shared prosperity. After all, we're all in the same boat - or, in this case, on the same ship. Let's make the journey a good one.

Call to Action

Thank you for embarking on this captivating journey through maritime leisure in "Sailing Beyond the Horizon: Captivating Facts About Cruise Ships." We hope you've enjoyed discovering the fascinating facts and insights about these majestic vessels and the enchanting experiences they offer.

Suppose you found this book informative and entertaining. In that case, we invite you to share your thoughts with others by leaving a review on Amazon. Your feedback and reviews play a crucial role in helping other readers discover the wonders of this book and make informed decisions about their reading choices.

We value your opinions and appreciate your support. Your review will encourage us and inspire others to set sail on this exciting adventure through the world of cruise ships. Your words can make a difference and help this book reach a broader audience.

Don't hesitate to share your thoughts, whether about the breathtaking cruise destinations, the historical significance of cruise ships, or the innovative technologies shaping modern maritime leisure. Your review will be a beacon guiding fellow travelers and maritime enthusiasts into the enchanting world of cruise ships.

CALL TO ACTION

Thank you for being a part of this maritime voyage. We sincerely appreciate your time and consideration in leaving a review on Amazon.

Happy cruising!

Glossary of Nautical Terms

- **Aft**: Toward the rear (stern) of the ship.
- **Berth**: The bed or sleeping accommodation on a boat or the space allotted for a ship to dock in a harbor.
- **Bow**: The front end of the ship.
- **Bridge**: The location from which a vessel is steered and its speed controlled. The navigational center of the ship.
- **Deck**: The floor of a ship; each level of a ship is called a deck.
- **Galley**: The kitchen area of a ship.
- **Hull**: The main body of the ship that floats on the water.
- **Knot**: A measure of speed at sea. One knot is equal to one nautical mile per hour.
- **Port**: The ship's left side when facing the bow. It also refers to a harbor where ships dock.
- **Starboard**: The ship's right side when facing the bow.
- **Stern**: The back end of the ship.

Additional Resources for Further Reading

- "Cruise Ship Tourism" by Ross Klein: An in-depth look at the cruise ship industry, its economic impact, and its environmental and social implications.
- "Introduction to Marine Engineering" by D.A. Taylo: For readers interested in the technical aspects of ship design and construction.
- "Sustainable Tourism on a Finite Planet" by Megan Epler Wood: A thorough examination of the impact of tourism, including cruise tourism, on the environment and local communities, with suggestions for sustainable practices.
- Cruise Lines International Association (CLIA) website: Offers various resources, including industry research, training opportunities, and updates on regulatory issues.
- Maritime Executive Magazine: Provides news, commentary, and analysis on various maritime topics, including cruise ships.
- Maritime Connector: A website offering various resources on the maritime industry, including news, job postings, and vessel information.
- Seatrade Cruise New*: A reliable source for the latest news and developments in the cruise industry.

- International Maritime Organization (IMO) website: Offers information on international maritime law and regulations, including environmental impact and safety.

Resources

Boguslawski, A. (2009). Advanced Ship Design for Pollution Prevention: Proceedings of the International Workshop "Advanced Ship Design for Pollution Prevention," Split, Croatia, 23-24 November 2009. CRC Press.

Bonilla, D. (2018). Transport Infrastructure and Systems: Proceedings of the AIIT International Congress on Transport Infrastructure and Systems (Rome, Italy, 10-12 April 2017). CRC Press.

Babb, S. D. (2001). Cruise Operations Management: A Systems Approach. Cengage Learning.

Cruise Critic. (n.d.). Cruise Ship Reviews. https://www.cruisecritic.com/reviews/

Cruise Lines International Association (CLIA). (n.d.). Cruise Industry Overview. https://www.cruising.org/news-and-research/research/cruise-industry-overview

Cruise Industry News. (n.d.). Cruise Market Watch. https://www.cruiseindustrynews.com/cruise-market-watch.html

Cudahy, B. J. (2001). The Cruise Ship Phenomenon in North

America. Cornell Maritime Press.

Dowling, R. K., & Weeden, C. (2017). Cruise Ship Tourism. CABI.

Garay, L., & Canoves, G. (2011). Life Cycle, Sustainability and the Attractiveness of Tourist Destinations. CABI.

Klein, R. A. (2011). Cruise Ship Tourism. CABI.

Printed in Great Britain
by Amazon